MW01125574

Copyright © 2020 by Catherine Flynn Friedman

All rights reserved. This book or any portion thereof may not be reproduced or used in any manner whatsoever without the express written permission of the publisher except for the use of brief quotations.

Printed in the United States of America

First Printing, 2021

Paperback ISBN 978-0-578-82538-0

The GLOWING RECTANGLE

written by
Katie Friedman

illustrated by
Anna Koprantzelas

Your grown-ups love you, this I know.
But every so often you'll see a glow.

From their palm you see that light,
distracting their mind and their sight.

Looking down with their eyes a-glaze
and an empty look upon their face.

They're off in a faraway distant land
thanks to the phone that's in their hand.

Is it the reason they don't want to play?
What are they doing on it all day?

Well, a phone connects us
to family and friends.
Its usefulness has no ends.

It can make music and play it too
or give directions to the zoo.

Phones have videos and funny games
(you'll see those when you fly on planes).

9

It's a little computer in their pocket,
more powerful than the world's first rocket.

But it's probably their work, I'd have to say -
they have a job, which comes with pay.

That money buys the things you need
like food and shelter and books to read.

So it might be tough to disconnect
if work is breathing down their neck.

13

They have an urge to check A LOT,
to see if it's important or not.

It's the most addicting thing you'll find,
(a lot like sugar but for your mind).

15

But there are lots of things a phone can't do -
it can't feel a hug from you.

The phone can't run, jump, joke or laugh.
It's not as fun as a bubble bath.

It can't hide, seek, skip or hop.
It won't tickle you until you drop.

The phone can't swing or climb up rocks
and it will never play with building blocks.

And even though they're trying their best,
sometimes their priorities are put to the test.

So pinky promise, right here and right now
(which is the very same as a solemn vow).

Make up a secret word or sign,
then use it to say what's on your mind.

A secret signal that will make them think
if there's really a work crisis on the brink.

And if there is not, they do solemnly swear
to put the phone down right then and right there.

To play with you and only you
because that's the best thing a phone can't do.

23

When you want to talk or have fun -
you're always priority number one!

25

CPSIA information can be obtained
at www.ICGtesting.com
Printed in the USA
LVHW071404130421
684372LV00007B/120

9 781087 927749